Burn Rate

A True Story of Greed,
Incompetence, and Start-Ups
by
Mick Theebs

Copyright © 2022 by Mick Theebs

July 1, 2022

ISBN: 978-1-7325503-4-6

Spiral Press
Greenwich, CT

All rights reserved. This book or any portion thereof may not be reproduced or used in any manner whatsoever without the express written permission of the author except for the use of brief quotations in a book review or scholarly journal.

> "Thinking to get at once all the gold the goose could give, he killed it and opened it only to find nothing."
>
> -Aesop

For everyone stuck in a trap and trying to get out.

Author's Note

All the names have been changed in this story to protect the guilty and innocent alike. The following series of events are true to the best of my knowledge and memory.

This is a story about the arrogance, incompetence, and greed that is the fabric of start-up culture. I will acknowledge that no two start-up experiences are the same, but that there is a common thread running through all bad ones. Bad owners. Bad business plans. Bad people. Lies heaped on lies. Ethical corners cut and crimes committed to keep the engine running. Enjoy this tale at your own risk and take careful heed of the lessons contained. Perhaps my own hardship can prevent the same from happening to someone else.

-Mick Theebs, 2022

Chapter I

I knew I was going to be fired. As soon as my boss mentioned potential cutbacks, I knew I was on the chopping block. Immediately after the standup meeting concluded, I marched straight upstairs to my grand-boss Janet's cube and asked her if I should be worried about getting laid off. I wasn't bad at my job, but I wasn't particularly good at it either. I damn sure didn't care about it. It was hard to be passionate about giving surgeons expense reimbursements for attending "conferences" in party cities like Miami and Las Vegas, all set up and sponsored by one of the biggest surgical device manufacturers in the world. Janet looked at me and told me with sincere apology that she had no idea and that I should prepare for the worst. I went back to my desk with a mixture of fear and excitement.

I hated my job. Aside from the fact that I was making good money, more money than I had ever made in my life at that point, there was very little to appreciate about my situation. I was a temp worker, so I was not considered an "official" part of the team. I had no benefits, no paid time off. The work I was doing was less than meaningless- it perpetuated a system of legalized bribery by giving already wealthy surgeons free vacations to pimp surgical devices. I had to come in every day wearing a tie, slacks, and nice shoes to sit at a computer and log numbers and answer emails. Aside from two very cool people who I got to chat with once in a while, I had no friends in the office. So, getting fired was not the end of the world for me.

I was 24 years old. I had no wife, no children. No mortgage, just rent to pay. I had a bunch of money saved up. Quitting my job was a daily fantasy. I wanted to get out and start my own business writing and editing. To try to cut my own path of making a living without answering to someone else. Without making someone else rich on the back of my own hard work. And it looked like the opportunity was finally presenting itself.

A few weeks later my boss, a nervous woman named Fran, came over to the desk they had wedged in a hallway between two filing cabinets and asked me to come speak with her in a conference room. I knew what was about to happen. She looked pale and distraught when I sat down across from her as if she were the one facing the firing squad. She began with a long preface about how great of a job I was doing and how everyone there really liked me (which was news to me) and said that it was strictly a result of the company laying off literally every single temporary worker that they had to let me go. She braced herself as I stared across the table at her. I shrugged and told her that it was fine, that I understood, and that it was nothing personal and probably for the best. The look of relief on her face was priceless. She told me that I could file for unemployment and they wouldn't dispute the claim, as if that was somehow a personal favor she was doing me. I told her I appreciated it and I left the building a free man.

About six weeks before this, I was named the very first Poet Laureate of Milford, Connecticut, my hometown. There was a bit of hubbub about this appointment. My face was on the front page of the local newspaper and I even did a little interview about who I was and what my goals were as Poet Laureate. I quickly learned that nobody had any idea what I was actually supposed to do aside from composing the occasional poem.

My friend, Jean-Michel, was speaking at our old high school and asked me to come and be his opener since I had just landed this fancy new position. Since I didn't have a job anymore, I was able to go with him. I was leaving the school after a morning of helping my friend inspire the youth when I ran into Brett Barber in the parking lot and we got to talking.

I had known Brett a long time. A long, long time. My first encounter with Brett was in elementary school. He was a grade above me and our teachers had the bright idea of pairing the older kids up with younger reading buddies for a day. Brett was my reading buddy. On top of that, Brett also lived in the same neighborhood as me and would occasionally take the same bus home from school with me. We didn't really get to know each other very well until high school though when we both were on the wrestling team.

Back in high school, Brett was basically my total opposite. He was huge, well over six feet tall, broad-shouldered, strong as an ox, and about as clever as one. Despite his lack of book smarts, Brett oozed charm and was very rarely struck speechless or unsure of what to say, which made him quite popular with everyone. He was also more than a little bit of a shithead with a cruel sense of humor and a nasty temper.

I was, on the other hand, a spindly little nerd. Skinny, even for someone as short as me. I was very smart but completely guileless when it came to social skills. I was occasionally good for a joke, but more often than not I was just loud and annoying and overbearing mostly out of that desperate teenage need to be accepted by my shithead peers. Brett and his friends, mostly his friends, would occasionally bully me when we were growing up. It wasn't anything like stealing my lunch money or putting my head in a toilet. Just lobbing whatever lame-ass insult they could muster and generally making me feel like an outsider who didn't belong whenever the mood struck them.

That was all a long time before fate thrust us together in that high school parking lot. I had grown considerably since then and I assumed that he had too. At first, I was just making chit-chat with Brett because it was the polite thing to do. He congratulated me on my appointment as Poet Laureate and asked me a little about my writing and what I was doing for work. I told him I was trying to start my own business writing for people. He, coincidentally (there are no such thing as coincidences), told me that he was trying to find a writer to help him with this new project he was working on and was wondering if I was interested. I told him I was, and we exchanged numbers and made plans to meet to discuss things further.

We met at Café Atlantique, this cute fixture of Milford, Connecticut, where locals would go on first dates, catch up with old friends, and discuss business opportunities. It was a relatively small place with as many tables squeezed into the U-shaped building as the fire marshal would allow. Brett was sitting at a table at the furthest point away from the front door and counter, on the other end of the U.

I joined Brett at his table and tossed my extremely overpriced messenger bag into an empty seat. Brett was wearing a wrinkled red polo shirt with the name of a landscaping company embroidered on the breast. He did not rise to greet me, though he did extend a hand past the open lid of his laptop to shake my hand and smile, seeming genuinely happy to see me.

I wore a collared shirt and slacks to try to balance the informality of our past relationship and the present possibility of doing business together. The shirt was a little tight on me and I smoothed it out before sitting down, feeling a little foolish when I saw how Brett had dressed.

We got to talking. He congratulated me on my appointment again and asked me what, exactly, a Poet Laureate is supposed to do. At that point, I had gotten so used to answering that question that I already had a prepared answer. I then told him a little bit about my employment situation and how I was looking to start my own writing business. Feeling a little insecure and nervous, I then steered the topic of conversation away from myself and asked him about what he had been doing. He told me a little about the landscaping company that he owned, gesturing with pride to the name stitched over his heart, and told me that it was the third-largest landscaping company in Milford. I congratulated him on the achievement, unsure how else to respond. He went on to tell me that he was reaching a point where the landscaping company was able to run independent of his guidance and that he was finally able to get working on a project he'd been dying to start for years.

There was a pregnant pause. I took a sip of my coffee to fill the quiet. Then he continued, his voice dropping slightly as if he were letting me in on some close-guarded secret. He said that when he was in college, he had an idea for a web-based service that would coach people on how to behave in a job interview. Clients would pay to do a video interview with people who have experience hiring folks and then get a report card telling them where they succeeded and where they needed improvement.

It wasn't a bad idea. To this day, I still don't think that it's a bad idea. I didn't fall out of my chair or do a backflip, but I was intrigued. I asked him how far along this project was. With an air of cool detachment, he told me that he already had a website up and running (which he pulled up on his laptop) and that his business partner was a veteran recruiter with almost three decades of experience ready to start giving mock interviews. He added that he was looking for someone to help with marketing, specifically by writing blog posts.

It wasn't anything I couldn't handle. I had run a variety of blogs on and off over the course of the mid-2000s and was, at that point, running my own art website that was pulling down a couple thousand views a month. I told him that was definitely something I could help with and he seemed quite pleased. I offered to write him a sample post to see how he liked my work and we could go from there. He immediately accepted. He asked me what my rates were.

I took a drink from my basically empty cup to stall while I screamed internally. I had no idea what to charge. The idea of someone not only wanting to pay me for my writing but asking me to name my price was entirely alien to me. I had done a little research on the subject but had no firm numbers. Moreover, my complete inexperience with these kinds of negotiations meant that I severely undervalued my time and labor, as I did not consider taxes and expenses. I told him that I'd put together a proposal for him that would include my rates in addition to the sample blog post. We parted ways not long after that, each of us plainly pleased with how this meeting had gone.

I went home to celebrate, which meant smoking a bunch of weed and playing video games. My roommate, Ted, came home not long after and I excitedly told him about how my meeting with Brett had gone. Ted, who had gone to high school with us, was also familiar with Brett and was less than thrilled for me. But, ever the good friend, Ted remained supportive and congratulated me, probably a little relieved that I was going to be able to pay my share of the rent without any trouble (not that he wouldn't have loaned me the money in a second if I had asked for it).

Chapter II

Emboldened by my early success, I tried to brainstorm other ways to drum up business. Almost immediately, I figured out that freelance sites like Fiverr were hardly worth a damn. It was a giant race to the bottom and there was simply no way I was going to be able to compete with people who were willing to be paid literal pennies on the dollar. I realized that I needed to go out into the real world and try to find clients in person. I figured that Yale, which was only a 30-minute drive from my house, would be a good place to try to rustle up some work since it was full of wealthy privileged students who could pay a ringer to punch up their essays for them. I made some fliers with a cheesy forgettable joke and my contact information and posted them all over the Yale campus. As I was walking back to my car, I passed a place that advertised tutoring services and went inside to see if I could find some projects to work on there. Coincidentally, they were in need of someone to help students with their writing, as their business was a service that helped wealthy Chinese students get into American prep schools and colleges and many of their clients did not have a perfect grasp of English. I gave the office manager my business card and he, in turn, gave me the card of one of their counselors who would provide me with a sample text to review.

I left New Haven feeling like Alexander the Great. I was on a roll and could not be stopped. Two for two on clients, both with a distinct possibility of it leading to steady work. Of course, my luck would run mostly dry after that with the occasional odd project popping up once in a while, but these two lines were plenty to support myself and my modest post-undergrad lifestyle of drinking, smoking, playing video games, and going into the city to see my girlfriend.

Over the next few days, I teased out a blog post for Brett and his new company. I poured over SEO guides and the best way to structure blog posts, learning all about keywords and word counts and subheadings and which way to face when praying to Google to get your webpage as high up on the search results list as possible. The actual content of the post was a cobbled-together list of interview tips I scavenged from the internet all streamlined and bundled together with my own spin and voice.

 Brett loved it. Though, in honesty, I think Brett would have loved anything I sent him. He wasn't exactly a wordsmith and I think was just relieved to have someone else he could foist this work onto. But I was more than happy to have this work foisted on me because I had also done some research on how much I should be paid and came up with 20 cents a word for writing blog posts, 15 cents a word for copy editing, and 20 bucks an hour for generic consulting work. Considering a blog post ran at least 300 words (per the SEO style guides) I was pulling down at least 60 bucks a post, which I could rattle off in less than an hour if I focused. It wasn't a bad deal at all and Brett found the terms agreeable as well.

 In exchange, Brett asked me to sign a non-disclosure agreement, something I had never been asked to do before. He emailed it over to me and I skimmed it. All I could glean from the dense legalese was that if I were to divulge "trade secrets" learned in my time working with him, I'd get slapped with a lawsuit. I signed it and sent it back over to him without a second thought. After all, Brett and I, if not actual friends, were at least friendly. I couldn't imagine a situation between us getting so bad that a lawsuit would be seriously considered.

 Once he got the NDA back, Brett wanted me to meet his business partner and we set up another meeting at Café Atlantique. I wasn't so nervous this time. Rather, I was excited. I was mixing it up with another young business owner, one infinitely more successful than I was. I was free, wheeling and dealing and trying to carve out a living for myself. Of course, the unemployment money was helping to float me and I had plenty saved to fall back on if the going got tough, but I was optimistic.

 When I got to Brett's usual spot in the back of the café, I saw that he was sitting with a much older man, one who looked old enough to be our father. Brett introduced him as Phil Mager. He was short and stocky with a shaved head and a wide grin. He had a low, gravelly voice that left his mouth in a grumbling croak. Despite his rough edges, he had an aura of friendliness about him that made him seem less gruff and more like a fun-loving uncle.

I shook his hand and sat down and frowned as the last name reverberated in my memory. I asked Phil if he had any children and he said he had a daughter, Joy, and a son, Derick. I realized that his son was dating my younger sister's friend. The link between our families smoothed any lingering awkwardness that might've existed between us as we got to talking.

Phil went into detail about his experience working as a recruiter. I listened and nodded and prompted with questions at lulls. I then took my turn to tell him all about myself and how I can help them grow as a business. At the time, I thought I was participating in a job interview, but in hindsight, it seemed more like they were trying to sell the company to me.

We got to talking about their business though we kept veering off into other stories and anecdotes. Brett brought up how he recently attended a baseball game and met the world record holder for most foul balls ever caught. Somehow, he convinced this guy to endorse this company that he'd never heard of on video, which Brett showed me in all its shaky, grainy glory. He said he wanted to post it on their website.

My brain lit up. I told him that he had just given me an idea for a post about how this person is a role model for people who are on the job search. I rattled off some key points and excitedly asked them what they thought. Brett and Phil shared a glance and Brett told me that he liked the idea and that I should write it up.

Over the next few days, I hammered out an article following the SEO guidelines handed down to me from a handful of Google searches. Once it was finished, I emailed it over to Brett and told him it was ready to be posted on the website's blog. He responded by telling me that he'll have an account made for me so that I can upload it myself as he was too busy to manage all the minutiae of copying and pasting text into a WordPress post. It didn't make much of a difference to me. If anything, I preferred not having to deal with Brett in this capacity. I'd write my posts, publish them, log the invoice in Quickbooks.

Once I had my login, I was cruising. Brett and I came to an agreement where he committed to two to three blog posts a week, which was not an insubstantial amount of money for me at the time. I spent a chunk of my savings on putting together an LCC through Legal Zoom. Unfortunately, because I was young and stupid and had no idea what I was doing, I ended up getting fleeced by Legal Zoom on the business equivalent of options and undercoating. I dropped several hundred dollars on services I had no use for in the slightest. A tele-accountant, a "registered agent service" (which was basically just a mailing address), and probably a bunch of other stuff I don't remember and definitely didn't need.

I could thankfully float myself on my unemployment payments, but I wasn't sure at the time about the ethics or legality of accepting unemployment money while also earning money as a freelancer. Once the work in New Haven with the Chinese international students began to pick up, and pick up it did, I made the (incredibly regrettable) decision that it would be best to forgo accepting any more unemployment money to avoid any potential legal or tax trouble. I made this decision partially on Brett's advice, who was becoming something of a mentor to me. Though he was technically my boss, I saw him as more of a peer. We were two small business owners working together, though I was basically only a business on paper and on the website I had built. He was clearly successful, as his landscaping company was running well enough to give him the time and money to be able to start something completely different, so I figured his advice would get me where I wanted to go.

I wasn't making as much as I was when I was working as a temp, but I was making plenty to survive on in a fraction of the time and that was worth it to me. After all, money is nice, but can a price be put on having the freedom to wake and sleep whenever I wanted? If I felt like screwing off and not looking for more clients or procrastinating on my existing projects, who was going to crack the whip? Some people do not have the temperament or discipline for such freedom, but I quickly found that I did.

This is not to say that things were perfect all the time. It was stressful to live in what was effectively a constant state of precarity. I had health insurance through my parents, but my 26th birthday wasn't that far away and I did not earn enough money to secure any sort of plan, even the most bare bones and "affordable" one available. I had no paid time off. No sick days. No retirement plan. If I needed or wanted anything to help do my work better, I had to find it, install it, and most importantly pay for it myself. The highs were high, but damn were the lows low.

Chapter III

    Brett gave me a call one afternoon and asked me if I could come over to his house and help him with something. I wasn't up to anything so I accepted. It was all billable hours, so it didn't matter much to me. In any case, I had never been to Brett's house before so I thought it would be cool to see what his living situation was like. The way a person keeps their house says a lot about them. Brett's house was… well, there's no way to describe it without being rude. It was a pit. The house itself had seen better days, but Brett's skills as a housekeeper were nonexistent. I wasn't expecting Buckingham Palace. My own house is a little cluttered and dirty, especially when I'm not expecting company, but this was on an entirely different plane of messiness. Half-empty beers littered the counters with spent cans spilling from the recycling. Empty bottles of liquor towered over them with shot glasses crusted to the counter. The walls were dingy and bare without any kind of decoration.
    The living room was a disaster area with a colossal television taking up roughly half of the floor space and a beat-up sectional sofa taking up most of the other half. The couch blocked the main entryway save for a narrow path that allowed people to circle around to enter the room. On one of the patches of floor that wasn't covered with clothes or workout equipment or miscellaneous junk was a half-eviscerated thirty rack of Bud Light sitting next to a coffee table covered with a full ashtray, empty beers, and a water bottle full of brown liquid someone was using as a spitter.
    I hid my shock behind a wall of politeness. Brett mumbled an apology about the mess and let me in, explaining that his roommates had thrown a party the night before. The floor was sticky as he led me to his bedroom, which thankfully was in slightly better shape than the rest of his house. It was a small room with just enough space for a bed, a desk, and a couple of dressers. Photos of family and friends and younger versions of himself hung on the

walls. Trophies and plaques sparkled in the gray light of the late autumn afternoon. A guy about my age sat on the bed writing on a legal pad. Brett sat down at his desk and introduced me to George.

George was tall and had a weathered but boyish face. Apparently, we were in the same high school class though I had never seen him before in my life. He wore glasses and had scruff that was starting to advance into proper beard territory. One of his arms was inked up with a full sleeve of hyper-realistic portraits of Abraham Lincoln and Albert Einstein and probably more I couldn't see hidden under his shirt. He had a kind of nervous energy about him. He smiled wide and gave my hand a firm shake when we were introduced, but there was an undercurrent of franticness in his geniality as if he were an actor on an audition for a part he desperately wanted. I threw down my bag and took a seat next to him on the bed.

We were working on an ambassador program for his start-up. Because the company's target demographic was students in college who have little to no experience, Brett thought it would be a good idea to set up a program where college kids could essentially sell his company's services to one another and rack up rewards for themselves. It was basically a pyramid scheme. Of course, I didn't point this out to Brett because I was trying to get paid, though I had a strong feeling that he would have a very difficult time recruiting potential ambassadors for a company that nobody has ever heard of. I didn't feel that it was my place to point out the logistical and optical problems of this program because I did not know how far along his business was, nor did I know how many existing clients he had already. It wasn't that Brett was deceptive or cagey about the numbers, it was more that he exuded so much confidence that it never occurred to me to question him. He seemed happy with how things were going, so who was I to question steady paying work?

We worked in fits and bursts. We would focus intently on the project at hand for a stretch of fifteen to twenty minutes, then Brett or George would get a phone call they'd have to take and throw us off our rhythm. Brett was on one such call when I started trying to chit-chat with George and get to know him better. I learned that he had a younger sister who was good friends with my sister, which didn't come as a surprise to me because both of my sisters are social butterflies who know basically everybody. I also learned that George was Brett's right-hand man for his landscaping business and was in charge of making sure all of the jobs went smoothly. I asked George how he got mixed up in this new project if he was also in charge of running Brett's other business and he told me that he was also an investor in the company because he thinks it's a good idea and wants to help it succeed however he can.

    We wrapped up our work for the day and parted ways. Aside from posting my blog posts two to three times a week, I didn't see much of Brett and George toward the end of the year because I was logging a ton of hours in New Haven. I was helping them review students' college essays and the deadline for most applications was the first of the year. We worked at a grueling miserable pace. I survived on energy bars and cheap weed and Canadian Club through that awful stretch, but I earned a healthy amount of cash and was offered a tutoring job in the spring for my trouble, which I accepted.

    When I finally survived that ordeal, I resurfaced in the new year with cash in my pocket and steady work lined up for me. Between the blog posts, editing, and the handful of consulting hours for Brett and the tutoring in New Haven, I was making enough to comfortably survive. I was still looking for work and side projects, but there was less urgency. I took time for myself. I worked on my own projects, spent time with my friends, visited my girlfriend in the city. Things were good. But as it usually goes when things are going well for someone, I got greedy.

Chapter IV

It had been a couple weeks since I had last seen or spoken to Brett. Between the regular chaos of the holidays and the added strain of working absurdly long hours workshopping overprivileged students' college essays, we both were focused on our own things. I gave Brett a call to see how he was doing and if he wanted to meet up. Considering winter was a slow time of year for landscaping (though they did do snow removal and plowing) I figured he'd be around. I was surprised when he told me that he was super busy and unable to meet up with me at a reasonable hour. However, he did say I can come with him to a local business organization's meeting that started at the ass crack of dawn, sweetening the pot by adding that it'd be a great networking opportunity and I'd probably be able to chase down more writing work there.

So, I dragged myself out of bed for a meeting at 7:30 in the morning. It was in the basement of this church right near the world-famous Milford, CT duck pond. I didn't know where I was supposed to be and I definitely did not want to go in alone, so I stood around in front of the church in the morning chill waiting for Brett's cherry red pickup truck to pull up. Thankfully, he was not late and came strolling over to me. We shook hands and said hello but didn't linger outside.

The church basement was like every church basement on Earth. A wide-open space, kind of dingy, with old folding chairs and tables. They were arranged in a large U. I was surprised to see that there were a few other people already sitting with their meeting materials in front of them. Most importantly, there was a table with a box of coffee and donut holes on the far side of the room, where most of the other attendees were milling around. It took a lot of self-control not to run across the room over there and start drinking coffee straight from the box. It was so early that I hadn't even gotten a chance to make myself any. Instead, I calmly walked over there with Brett and poured myself a cup with a donut hole for good measure.

Brett immediately started chit-chatting with some of the people there he knew and introduced me as his guest. I didn't know it at the time, but it was a big deal to bring a guest to this meeting. That is, it was something that allowed in very specific circumstances as they had a very rigid set of rules and procedures to follow. When I say rigid, I mean rigid. Like every person was given two minutes to introduce themselves, enforced by timer. If someone bumped up against the limit, they would get cut off by the meeting facilitator, who was the president of that organization's branch. I had never been in such an environment before and didn't know what to make of it. On the one hand, I respected the strict sense of order they had cultivated, but on the other, I thought it was also strange and a little too rigid for my tastes as a freewheeling artistic type.

I introduced myself with little difficulty. Public speaking has never been much of a problem for me as long as I didn't have to memorize exact lines to say. Some eyebrows went up when I mentioned I was a writer and I could tell that they were interested in my services, which was the entire purpose of the group in the first place. It was a place where small business owners could refer business to one another. After everyone went around and said their bit, one person got up and got to talk at length about their services and how great their business was and the entire thing was a complete bore. The meeting ended not long after and everyone hung around to talk and network a little.

Brett melted into the pack, leaving me on my own. I would have been annoyed but almost immediately someone came over to me to talk about my writing and how we could do business together. I ended up talking to a few people about some potential paying assignments when the president of the club came over to me with a paper in hand. I already knew he was there to sell me on membership, so I was willing to listen to his pitch. Considering the response I was already getting, I could see myself getting up early once a week to rustle up some business. That is, I saw myself doing that until I saw the price tag for membership. Eight hundred dollars a year. In terms of business expenses, that may not seem like a huge amount of money. But to a 24-year-old freelancer who was barely paying the bills, that was a fortune.

Eventually, it was time to go so Brett and I walked out together. He asked me what I thought about the group. I told him that it was interesting but there was no way that I could afford it. He nodded in understanding and agreed that it was a lot to pay up front, but that it could pay for itself in time. I told him that I had dropped almost the same amount of cash on getting my LLC put together. I thought his eyes were going to pop out of his head. He couldn't believe that my LLC fees cost as much as they did and that I should have just told him that I was trying to form an LLC and he would have set me up for a fraction of a price. I shrugged and told him that there was no taking it back now. I asked him if he wanted to know what business name I went with and told him that I wanted to call my business Perfectionist Media.

Brett considered the name for a moment then told me that he wasn't a fan. I was honestly a little crushed. After all, Brett wasn't just my first real client as a freelancer/business. He was also a mentor. He was one of the only people I knew my age that had started a successful business. His approval meant a lot to me then. I asked him what he didn't like about the name and he just shrugged and said it didn't do it for him. Then he shook my hand, said goodbye, and got into his truck, leaving me to walk back to my car.

After some brief consideration, I stuck with the name solely because I couldn't think of anything better. I liked the name. I thought it represented the type of writer and creator I was: someone who strove to get things exactly right for my clients. Brett's casual dismissal of that stung.

Chapter V

A few days after that meeting, Brett gave me a call. He told me that he hired someone to help run the social media accounts for his website and that he wanted us to work together. He sent me over the contact information of someone named Jason. I sent him a text introducing myself and we set up a video call to meet "face to face" because he was living in California.

Jason was younger than me with long dark hair and square handsome features. His voice was low and hoarse, due in no small part to how much weed he smoked. Jason had a kind of reserved energy about him. He didn't speak much, but I could tell he was always thinking. At first, I wasn't sure what to make of this kid because of that cool-bordering-on-cold exterior. I was a little worried he was going to try to edge me out of the business.

As we got to talking, he thawed out a little. He told me how he got connected with Brett through his father, who knew Brett's father. Like me, we both grew up knowing him. Like me, he loved smoking weed and had a taste for video games. I was relieved to find that he specialized in social media marketing and that he was glad to have someone help him out by writing blogposts and creating content for him to share. We pulled up a calendar and planned out a month's worth of blog posts and talked about what else we were working on. One thing he mentioned needing was a steady supply of photos to post on these various accounts, which I was more than happy to help provide him with since I had invested in a stock photo account for the blog posts already. He asked me how much they would cost, and I told him I'd have to do some math and get back to him on that.

I figured that since it took me some time to track down and compile whatever photo Jason needed, I'd bill for .25 an hour per photo, which comes to five bucks a photo. Certainly, this was not a great price for a stock photo, but I needed to be paid for my time and cover the expenses of the stock photo account. In my defense, there are stock photo websites that charge more than five dollars a photo but trick people into paying more by first converting dollars into their version of company scrip. I sent the rate to Jason and thought that was that.

I was playing video games with my friends one afternoon a few days later when I got a call from Brett. He was furious at the price I was charging him for the photos. He was yelling at me about how much business he had given me and how the thanks he was getting in return was getting gouged for stock photos. Brett had never spoken to me like that before. To make matters worse, I was on mic with my friends and they could hear our entire conversation. I immediately quit the game and tried to smooth things over. I was terrified he would pull his business. After all, he made up about half of my income alone. He held my livelihood in his hands and he knew it. I told him how much I valued his business and our working relationship, gingerly trying to defuse the ticking timebomb of his temper. I also reminded him in the gentlest terms I could muster that he told me to buy a stock photo account for myself if I wanted it instead of having his company pay for it and that I needed to cover my costs on that if Jason was going to use the photos as well. He considered this in angry silence and finally said that I made a fair point, but five dollars a photo was too much, and declared that he would pay a dollar a photo. I told him that was fair and agreed to the terms without so much as a counteroffer, relieved that I was able to maintain the relationship.

In retrospect, I could see that Brett did not think of me as a separate business that he was buying services from but rather a contracted employee that he could browbeat and bully into doing what he needed. Of course, at the time I did not have the experience or the insight to understand this. I wish I had known at the time that this was the beginning of a disturbing pattern. It would have saved me a lot of trouble.

Chapter VI

While building this new business and crying broke the entire time, Brett bought himself a new house. I learned this when he called me up out of the blue, a habit that he was indulging more and more, and asked me to basically drop everything and come over and help him with some project he was working on. I told him I'd be at his house and he said that he had moved and gave me the new address.

It was a much nicer, bigger space than his old house. It appeared to be a beach cottage that someone had built an addition onto. It was wide and empty in that still-moving-in way. Boxes were piled in corners. Only the most essential pieces of furniture were haphazardly dropped in the center of rooms. The walls were blank and bare. It was interesting to see what Brett had prioritized on unpacking. The dining room table was set up, but there were no chairs, only two sets of red cups arranged in a pyramid on each end of the table with some Ping-Pong balls. There didn't seem to be any plates or silverware in the kitchen, but half-empty handles and shot glasses already littered the counter. I wondered how much of this mess Brett blamed on his roommates.

He told me to come upstairs into his bedroom. It was a modest little room about the same size as the one in his old house. The only difference was that there was a little sunporch that he had turned into a makeshift office. Taking up most of the space was his desk, which was covered with invoices and bank statements from the landscaping business. Behind it was a little table and chair that was meant to serve as a secondary desk.

Brett and George were in there both typing away at their keyboards. They both looked relieved when I came through the door. Brett told me to grab a chair from downstairs and take a seat, that they needed help with writing the welcome email for when people sign up to the website. After dragging a chair up the stairs and finagling it in that tiny space, I booted up my laptop and got to work. We had a nice rapport working together. I would fall into this frantic sort of flow state where the words would come tumbling out of me. Brett and George would occasionally toss suggestions my way, but for the most part, they let me do my thing as I worked myself up into a mania. It wasn't long before we had an email draft finalized.

  Once the creative haze in my mind cleared, I was a little surprised that they hadn't already put something together for this. I realized that I had no idea how many accounts were on the website or if they were even doing any business. Brett was very opaque about this information, though he always managed to project an aura of confidence and success. It was easy to get sucked into that and forget to ask important questions like "Is this business currently operational?" or "how much money do we have left to keep this project going?" Despite the obvious concerns that this realization brought up, I was still convinced that the idea was a winner and that Brett was a good enough businessperson to steer the ship. Of course, I was also making good money and I wasn't about to derail that gravy train with something as silly as the long-term viability of the company.

  Aside from planting a seed of doubt, this little work session gave me some more face time with George. He seemed like a good guy. Friendly enough, anyways. Still, I was kind of surprised when he invited me over to hang out a couple of days later. I didn't have much to do, and I figured it'd be a good idea to get to know one of the only other people working for Brett.

  He lived in his father's house not too far away from me. I could've walked or ridden my bike if I wanted to, but it was cold and I couldn't be bothered. He answered the door with a wide, nervous smile. The television was blasting One America News. A little black pug named Dennis was losing his mind when I came through the door and George was trying to quiet him down. Sitting in a Lazyboy recliner was George's dad, a weathered old dude who could have been anywhere from fifty to a hundred years old.

  For context, this was in early 2017, so everyone was still pretty shellshocked that Donald Trump had somehow managed to get elected president. There was a general air of tension because people all over were realizing that their coworkers, friends, and family members were racists, or at least willing to support an overt racist.

George introduced his dad to me, and he seemed polite enough despite being interrupted while having far-right propaganda beamed into his head. George and I sat down on the couch and George started rolling a joint while I made small talk with his dad. Almost immediately, things took a turn to politics as One America News was still filling the room with its garbage slurry stink. George's dad started going off about how the president needed to ban Muslims to keep us safe from terrorism. I pushed back in as polite of a manner as I could. Naturally, I wanted to tell this man that the news he was watching was full of shit and he was being racist, but I was a guest in his home and had literally just met him. George could tell that I was getting upset and suggested that we smoke the joint on a walk. I agreed and we took Dennis and the joint outside.

Once we got out of the house, George apologized profusely for his father. I told him it was no big deal as he lit up. I told him that I didn't really remember him from high school and asked him what he had been doing since then. He looked down as he passed the joint back over to me. I smoked and watched him work up the nerve to say whatever was on his mind. George told me that he had transferred out of our high school and into alternative education, which was probably why I didn't know him. He then went on to say that in the time between then and high school he had spent a stretch of time in prison.

I blinked. George did not seem like the type. He was so nervous and eager to please, it was hard to believe that he'd do wrong by anybody. I asked him what he had done to get himself in jail, figuring it was something stupid like getting caught pushing weed or something. He started his story by saying he was very young and stupid when this happened and then told me that he and his friend skipped school one winter day and they decided, on a whim, to snatch some old lady's purse. She tried to chase after them and slipped on some ice and got hurt. He ended up getting charged with theft and assaulting an elderly person and spent 3 years in prison. His shame was palpable. I puffed on the joint and then passed it over to him. I told him that that was a stupid and terrible thing he did, but he served his time and clearly learned a lesson from the experience, so the best thing to do was keep moving forward. He gave me a weak, flushed smile and hit the joint. As he exhaled, he told me how grateful he was for Brett, as it was very difficult for an ex-con like him with little skills or professional experience to find work. He went on to say that he was also very excited to be part of this new company that Brett was putting together and had invested some of his own money in the project as well.

    I was less enthusiastic about our work. I told him that I thought it was a good idea and I was ready to see where things go, but I was enjoying being able to set my schedule. That flexibility was key in being able to manage all my disparate projects. I was doing paid work for clients, tutoring in New Haven, working on my writing projects, and running my art website. George was almost in a state of disbelief at how much I was up to. I tried to encourage him to figure out what it was that he liked to do and pursue it. He seemed to appreciate it.

    We walked and talked for a little more. George did most of the talking from there as we worked to try to figure out what, exactly, George wanted to do with himself. He spent a lot of time working for Brett. I learned that he worked so much because his mother had passed away while he was in jail and it was mostly up to him to pay the mortgage, though they did rent one of the bedrooms out to one of George's friends to cover costs as well. I know it was probably rude, but I asked him what happened to his mother.

    It's probably wrong, or at least inconsiderate, but the first thought I have when I hear that somebody passed away is "how?". I was sad for George regardless because it's a terrible thing to lose a parent at such a young age, doubly so to be locked up in jail when it happens, but I still wanted to know how his mother passed away.

    He didn't seem to mind. He told me that, apparently, she just laid down for a nap on the couch and never woke up and that was it. He punctuated his short, sad story with a shrug. It seemed like he had made peace with it as just another cruel twist of fate, one of those things that just happens to people sometimes. Still, I expressed my condolences. What else is a person supposed to say in that situation? He thanked me for them and we kept walking.

Though it seems like our conversation was linear, I am only making sense of it now with hindsight. The truth is that our conversations had a kind of circular orbit. We would take turns talking about our personal lives but always would come back to the company. Our thoughts on it. Work that needed to be done. Upcoming projects. Goals. How good of a job we thought Brett was doing. It was a constant presence, the keystone of our relationship.

George's second favorite topic to discuss after work was his on-again/off-again girlfriend. She seemed to cause him quite a bit of stress and trouble. I mostly just listened and tried to offer him advice whenever I thought I had something useful to say, but it seemed to me that there wasn't much to salvage in the relationship and that George would be better off on his own. He knew that and admitted that it was true, but he just couldn't work up the strength to leave her. I sympathized. It's hard to be in love with someone who sucks the life out of you.

Chapter VII

I settled into a kind of routine where I would pen my weekly blog posts, have my calls with Jason to plan ahead, and occasionally go to Brett's house for some group work for a couple of hours one or two times a week. On one such occasion, I remember going to his house and up to his little makeshift office on the sunporch. Something was different about Brett. He was antsy and anxious and was speaking with urgency about this idea he had. He was very particular about what he wanted. It was going to be a Facebook ad with a photo of a skull or an atomic explosion or both with THIS WILL KILL YOUR JOB INTERVIEW in big red letters with a link to a blog post he wanted me to put together. The idea was, apparently, to scare people into joining up and buying mock interviews. The thing that stands out in my memory was Brett's odd behavior as we worked. It was almost like a manic episode, which I had unfortunately seen several close friends go through. Still, I was in no position to argue and helped put together the ad for him, though I couldn't help but feel like something was wrong. I chalked it up to just Brett being under a lot of pressure and wanting to see the company succeed.

    I was making good money. It seemed like the company was growing. Brett was very juiced up about this new business development person that seemed interested in what we were doing. She was a high-powered executive coming from sales for a blue-chip Fortune 500 company. She somehow found out what we were up to and decided she wanted to get in on the action. What's more, was that she was willing to work for free in exchange for equity in the company. She had some pretty ambitious goals as well, saying that she felt that she could generate hundreds of thousands of dollars in business in a short amount of time.

    This news, coupled with the fact that Jason was moving back to Connecticut from California to work with us, led me to believe that the company was on the verge of taking off in a big way. I was doing a lot of work for Brett at this point. Almost every piece of written material that the company was using had my fingerprints on them, either through copywriting or editing. And while I'm not proud of it, I was seeing dollar signs and getting worried that I was going to be left behind. So, I called Brett and asked to meet with him.

  We met at this wonderful restaurant in Milford called The Plate at Brett's request. As per usual, I had to adjust my schedule, which was admittedly more flexible, to suit his. When I came in, he was already seated at a table with a plate in front of him. I was incredibly nervous. To this day, I cannot explain why. After all, what I was asking for was not unreasonable. I wanted to become a bigger part of his company because I thought it was a good idea. I had a lot of skills to bring to the table and was already producing useful work for him. But at the time I didn't understand this about myself. I was deeply intimidated by our lopsided power dynamic in that Brett was the main source of my income and seemed to be aware of how much I depended on his business.

  I told Brett that I wanted to become more involved with his company and that I could see it was growing quickly and that I wanted a seat at the table. He looked up from his food with a blank expression and, playing dumb, asked me what that meant exactly. I told him that I wanted some equity in the company and was prepared to work for it. He looked down at his food and chewed slowly. Finally, he nodded and looked back up at me and said that he'd figure something out and get back to me in a few days. I hung around for a little longer and we talked about what else was going on in our lives. He told me about this new girl he met and seemed pretty excited about. I had never seen him so happy about a new relationship before. He was always sort of a player and I took it as a sign of growing up that he'd found a happy committed relationship for himself. I left the restaurant feeling about twenty pounds lighter and with a sense of optimism bordering on delirium.

  Brett called me up a few days later and asked me if I was still serious about getting more involved with his company. I told him that I was, trying to push down some of the nervousness that was bubbling up in my stomach. Ever since he called me and gave me hell over those stock photos, I was always a little anxious whenever Brett's name appeared on my phone. Most of the time, there was no reason for him to be upset and it was a completely irrational fear on my end, but I still was in a state of precarity and the last thing I needed was for Brett to yank the rug out from under me by pulling his work, so I wanted to keep him happy. At any rate, he told me to come to Phil's house tomorrow morning.

    I had never been to Phil's house before. It was a cozy little cape house that reminded me of my parent's house. I remember when I first walked through the front door, I saw a familiar face sitting on one of the couches. Jason was there in the flesh, slouched over his laptop in a position that I would come to find very familiar. I was shocked that he was already back in Connecticut. I greeted him excitedly and he seemed pleased to see me, though was much more reserved about it.

    I went into the kitchen where I could hear Brett and Phil talking. Phil's kitchen was pretty big, but most of the floor space was taken up by an enormous dining table. Brett and Phil were sitting at the table with George. Everyone had a laptop in front of them and they all were looking at Brett's phone which was on speakerphone. A woman's voice filled the space. She had a sharp, authoritative tone that commanded the room even after being filtered through the phone. I had never seen Brett listen so intently in my life.

    I set my things down as quietly as I could and listened in. I caught on that this was that hotshot business development person that he was telling me about, whose name was Christina. Not Christy. Not Tina. Christina. I found it fascinating that she chose to go by her full name and nothing else. It made it clear that she had little patience for nonsense, or at least that was the first impression it gave. Christina was talking about developing a sales team and how Brett needed to find some people to work under her.

    Brett said that it would take some time to build out the team more, but she could start with George and me, looking up from the phone expectantly at the two of us and adding the words right guys half a question and half a statement. I blinked, completely disarmed. Time slowed down. I had never worked in sales before in my life. I had no desire to. I had no previous knowledge about this decision. But at that moment, it was immediately clear to me that this was what Brett had in mind for me if I wanted a piece of the company and that there would be little use in arguing with him. Moreover, I was put on the spot and I didn't want to jeopardize the company's relationship with Christina and I definitely didn't want to come off as an asshole the first time speaking to the person meant to be my new boss. So, I cleared my throat, shrugged, and said I'd give it a try but I'd never worked in sales before and that my skills might be put to better use somewhere else.

  Christina didn't seem worried and said that she had lots of experience coaching people who are new to sales. The rest of the meeting went on though I was unable to focus. I was too busy thinking about my new future as a salesperson and how Brett had ambushed me with this new development.

Chapter VIII

I was still working with the international students in New Haven but managed to carve out some time for a conference call with Christina and George for training. As predicted, I was terrible at sales and George was no better. Christina first had us attempt to sell the program without any assistance to size us up. It wasn't long into our mock sales call that she put the brakes on and started coaching. It was clear that her work was cut out for her.

To her credit, Christina was nothing short of a patient and professional teacher. She walked us through our mistakes and taught us what to say. I remember pacing my bedroom floor with my phone pressed to my ear as I would alternate between being a salesperson and a customer with George as Christina occasionally interjected to give thoughts and advice. At first, I was pretty contemptuous of the entire process. I didn't want to be in sales. I wanted to write. But what I wanted more than even that was to own some equity in the company. After all, as George would tell me one day while we were smoking at his house, one thing investors found very promising about the company was the impressive catalog of blog posts on the website. I felt that I deserved a slice of the pie if I was the one creating all this potential value. It was this greed that forced me to endure the pain of contorting myself into a position I had no desire to be in.

One thing that helped me get acclimated to this new set of skills and responsibilities was to approach the sales process the same way that an actor approaches a new character. At the time, my friends and I were writing and starting to shoot a web series, so I was trying to hone my acting abilities. It did help to think of my sales script as a script for a performance. I was playing a character called "Salesman" and my character wanted to land a meeting and make a sale. Of course, looking back on it now it seems incredibly lame, but it was a very effective strategy at the time.

While this was going on, Brett had somehow managed to secure a television appearance on a local news station to talk about the company. I remember first watching it at George's house. I was floored by the fact that Brett was on the TV and did not pay close attention to what he was saying or how he was holding himself. I was excited for him and the company and by extension myself. In a way, it helped to justify the fact that I was now working sales instead of writing. After all, unsuccessful companies don't do television appearances.

Christina on the other hand was mortified at Brett's performance. He was wearing a wrinkled polo shirt and looked as if he had just rolled out of bed before walking on set. He was clearly unprepared when he made his remarks as it was meandering and full of filler words and vapid bullshit. Later, Brett confessed to us that he was up all night pounding energy drinks and Adderall the evening before he went on TV and had, in fact, just gotten out of bed before stepping on set. I remember we were at Phil's house talking about it while Brett was taking care of some landscaping stuff and Phil told said that his eldest daughter had seen the clip and asked if Brett had ever been on TV before. When she learned that he hadn't, she quipped that he should never go on again.

We collectively agreed that moving forward, Brett should under no circumstances appear on camera and that Christina should be the one to handle any sort of public appearances. This incident really changed the way I saw Brett. Until then, I looked up to the guy. After all, he was running a successful business and starting a new one at the same time. He radiated a confidence that created an illusion of competence and, while it quickly fell apart under scrutiny, it did provide significant cover for his lack of actual ability. This was the first time I'd seen Brett do a bad job. Though in truth, Brett didn't have many opportunities to show off his skills as a CEO aside from bringing people on to work and cutting us checks.

Chapter IX

Christina and I grew close in a relatively short period. Part of the reason why was that we spent a considerable amount of time together. She lived in the city and would commute to Connecticut one or two days a week on the train. I was usually the one to pick her up and drop her off. We'd make chitchat in the car or while we were waiting for her train to come and got to become friends.

With our sales training complete, it was time to put it into action. But before we did that, we needed to put together a database of potential customers. And simultaneously, we also needed to solidify our product offerings and their price points. This was something that Brett had put together, but it was in the slapdash way we had come to expect from him without much consideration for long-term strategy or the wider implications of such choices. So, we needed to take a second look at it and that meant I needed to write the copy for the new product offerings.

We ended up retooling and streamlining things significantly. We had started with six different types of interviews that were functionally indistinguishable from one another and pared it down to two services: a resume review and a mock interview with varying levels of post-interview reporting and resources. The critical thing we needed to address was the price. Christina was adamant that the prices that Brett had set were far too low and that was not just because she was paid on commission. The prices that Brett had set left very little room for overhead and meant that our "professional interview experts" would be getting paid something on the order of twenty bucks an hour to churn out three interviews. It was a sweatshop tactic that was not conducive to long-term scaling or success.

While they were figuring that out, I was going through the website updating all the copy. There were some typos and awkwardly worded statements, but nothing that was painfully wrong.

Brett had shelled out a lot of money for what was a relatively simple WordPress build with a member management system and a bunch of cosmetics all put together by a local graphic design firm. I didn't know how exactly much money he had funneled to them, but I knew that Brett was overpaying significantly. Jason and I had talked privately in our regular content planning meetings about how it would be much easier and cheaper to just knock up a simple Squarespace website with a scheduling plugin on a landing page. Of course, in hindsight, I should have realized that this was a massive red flag that Brett didn't think of this himself, and that it was a demonstration of his lack of technical proficiency. This was particularly alarming because he would often describe our scrappy little start-up as a "tech company" even though we fundamentally were a service company that just happened to use technology to provide our service.

  I would later learn that part of the reason why Brett branded our company as a tech company was because one of his mentors who was guiding him had founded a tech company of his own, some software as a service or something, and successfully sold it off to some giant corporation for a massive profit. Brett was trying to follow this mentor's model even though he was not a programmer, was operating a different business model with a different target market, and was generally unfamiliar with the market he was trying to reach. Red flags on red flags on red flags. As it turns out, when you're seeing dollar signs, you miss every warning that comes flying past you.

  While I was going through the website, Christina asked if we had any kind of mission statement up. I told her that we did not, but that was something that I could probably put together with little trouble. We decided it would be best to write one then and there. Normally when I wrote something for them, Brett or George would give me the gist of what they were trying to say, and I would put together something that would sound nice. Sometimes Brett would quibble over a word or two, but for the most part, they were pretty happy with my writing. Things were completely different with Christina in the mix. She was not so easily satisfied. As a result of her experience in the corporate world and her general demand for quality work, we spent at least ninety minutes laboring over what would ultimately become a single sentence. In all honesty, I appreciated having someone hold me to a higher standard of work. Christina had a way about her that is only found in the best coaches and teachers. She was able to push and demand the best from the people under her tutelage without creating any resentment or discomfort. It is something I appreciate about her to this day.

Unfortunately, everyone else did not feel the same. Brett in particular. I think he was threatened by Christina because she was so competent and seemed to know exactly which way to steer the ship, whereas Brett had kind of a meandering, seat-of-the-pants style of leadership. Of course, this is just speculation, but I think Brett knew that he was outclassed by her in just about every capacity. And instead of doing what a good leader would do and embrace all of the talent and skill and enthusiasm that Christina had and was able to foster, Brett became bitter and jealous and would occasionally butt heads with her.

They went back and forth over the price structures for a couple days. Brett even brought his mentor in to help. They worked on figuring out a price plan and Christina kept pushing him to increase the prices, telling him that we were going to be selling these to colleges and they had plenty of money to spare. Brett couldn't seem to wrap his head around this and kept trying to set lowball prices to get more direct user purchases. In the end, he did come around and they were able to put together a solid pricing plan.

While that was going on, George and I were working on building out our sales database. We created an excel spreadsheet of all the higher education institutions in a given state, starting with our home state of Connecticut and working our way first through New England and then the Mid-Atlantic area. We would log emails and phone numbers and the names of any potential decision-makers. It was a mind-numbing slog. The exact kind of task I would do at that horrible old temp job. It took several weeks to get a workable database going and because George often had to deal with Brett's landscaping company as well, I would often be left alone in Phil's kitchen to work on the database myself.

It was during this time that I got to know Phil a little better. He had been a recruiter for many years and was the brains behind the whole job skills part of the operation. At that point, he didn't have much to do for the business since we were trying to drum up clientele, so he would work on his own recruiting stuff and make chitchat and occasionally leave to go pick up his wife or attend to other business. But we would talk about the state of the business and prospects and things like that as well. He was always polite but had a distant quality about him.

One time, I remember, he asked me to give him a ride to the pawn shop. His wife had taken his car to work and he was stranded at his house. So, I gave him a lift and we went inside to pick up something he had pawned. A ring or a bracelet or some piece of jewelry. I remember how he bristled when I used the word "hocked" to describe what he had done. He icily informed me that there wasn't anything wrong with using a pawn shop to get a little bit of money and that they had a bad wrap in general. I was a little taken aback, as Phil had never been short with me before, but I didn't say anything else. I figured he must've had a lot on his mind if he was putting his possessions in hock for extra money.

Chapter X

Eventually, we got the database up and running with some janky off-brand CRM because Brett didn't want to spring for Salesforce. Christina took Brett's frugality in stride though it was clear that she thought the decision was penny wise and pound foolish. In any case, with the database full of prospects and our sales training complete, Christina decided that George and I were ready to actually make some calls.

It was a big day. For some reason, we had chosen a Friday to start, which we quickly learned was a terrible day to make sales calls as everyone is typically so burned out from the week that they do not have any patience for some schmuck calling them about a product that could potentially put them out of a job from a company they'd never heard of before. The air was full of tense anticipation in Phil's house that day.

George and I were each given our separate areas to work in. He got the sitting room near the kitchen and I got Phil's daughter's old bedroom. Our job was to make calls and set meetings for Christina to pitch our company in person. I remember sitting down with my laptop and my headphones and dialing the first call, trying to forget that Christina was on the other side of the door listening. It went to voicemail. So, I dialed the next number. Voicemail.

As it turns out, lots of people working in higher education knocked out early on Friday afternoon. I did eventually get someone on the phone. The call went fine, from what I can recall. I asked them about what services they offer and if they give students mock interviews. The person on the other line was a little confused because they thought I was a student at first and got annoyed when they realized that I was a literal telemarketer. Things picked up a little from there. I didn't end up setting any in-person meetings but I did manage to get a follow-up call on the books.

George, on the other hand, managed to set an in-person

meeting. I'll admit that I was disappointed that I wasn't the one to set our first meeting as silly as that might be. But I was happy for George and our company as a whole, as it meant that we were one step closer to blowing up and getting rich.

To celebrate, Christina insisted we all went out and had drinks in downtown Milford at a bar called Citrus. It was a dim room with plenty of seating that was always busy but never packed. We took a booth in the back corner of the bar and got started. We were all there: Me, George, Christina, Jason, Phil, Phil's wife Maxine, and Brett. There was a sense of delirious joy around that table as we pounded beers and took shots and toasted the future of our company. At one point Christina thought it would be nice if we went around the table and each said something nice about Brett.

When my turn came up, I told everyone about the first time we had met in elementary school and how I never would guess that I'd be working with him at a start-up he founded, conveniently leaving out the part of how for most of the time growing up together Brett was a massive shithead whose friends took immense pleasure in bullying me. Finally, after we each took our turn sucking up to the boss, Brett wanted to say a few words.

He spoke about the company and how strongly he believed in its future success and how grateful he is to have everyone involved to help build his vision. He stressed that we faced a particularly unique challenge because we were a "true start-up". He clarified by saying we were not just attempting to start a new business, we were attempting to create an entirely new sector to do business in. He raised his glass of aged scotch when he was finished speaking and we all drank.

In retrospect, I realize that Brett was entertaining delusions of grandeur. After all, it wasn't like the idea of helping someone hone their skills with a mock interview was revolutionary. Nor was the idea of doing it over Skype. Nor was attempting to get in on the massive amounts of money that colleges and universities had at their disposal. So, there wasn't anything special about what we were doing at the core of the idea. But for reasons that escape me even today, Brett thought we were onto some really groundbreaking stuff with this business.

But it was a fun night and the high-water mark of our entire time as a company. There was a real sense of camaraderie that night. It felt like we were a fingertip away from closing our fists around money, power, prestige- everything each of us wanted. We pounded shots and chased with long sips of mixed drinks. At one point, Christina and I were talking alone. She looked at me with glassy eyes and said that she wanted to ask me something and then went on to ask me why I had such a chip on my shoulder about sales. I was a little surprised at the question. I wasn't shy about my feelings about being roped into sales. I was resentful of the entire sales process and felt it was, ultimately, not the best use of my talents as a writer. Moreover, the incentives that Brett had set up for me were pitiful. Ten bucks a meeting set and not a single cent cut from the resulting end deal. Christina told me that I was good at sales, a natural, and that I could make a lot of money if I put my mind to it. The thing was, I didn't want to put my mind to it at all and was just holding out until I got my equity in the company. Of course, I didn't tell her that. I just shrugged and told her that I'd think about what she said. And the rest of the night continued in a drunken blur.

The high was short-lived. Brett was starting to become more antsy about how many hours we were logging and how much money we were spending as a company. He was always cheap, but he was getting cheaper by the day. He was paying Phil some money, a nominal amount most likely, to let us work in his house, he was paying for the relatively modest tools that Christina needed, and he was hemorrhaging money with the design company. He was on the hook for a bunch of cash with them, which made no sense if you looked at the quality of our website. It was fine, but definitely not worth tens of thousands of dollars. So, Brett worked out some kind of deal with the owner of the firm, I guess wiping out some of the debt in exchange for a chunk of the company. He was very opaque about the whole thing, but George would give me little scraps of information occasionally when we were working at his house. As a result of all this, though, Brett told us that we were going to have to take a pay cut, framing it as our end of the bargain to get the equity in the company that he was definitely, totally going to give us eventually at some point in the future that was potentially worth hundreds of thousands of dollars. So, my already modest rates were cut in half and I was earning minimum wage.

    I was quite bitter about this pay cut as it caused some problems for me. I was just skating by before he chopped my income in half. I was still tutoring in New Haven, which was very good money, but that only made up about a quarter of my hours worked each week. Most of my time was spent working for Brett. I hadn't tried to track down any new customers for my own business in months and I frankly did not have the time or energy to do so. But I wanted that equity. It was more than just greed. I had helped build Brett's company. Every scrap of writing passed through my hands before it was published on the website or in an email. I had helped build the company and felt entitled to a piece of it. So, I stayed on board even though the pay cut was devastating and made my life about a million times more difficult than it had to be.

Chapter XI

On we suffered. George and I worked phone calls into our weekly routines. We would occasionally work from his house if we didn't feel like going over to Phil's, or if Phil had some other business to take care of. If I didn't have to tutor, which wasn't often, I'd hang out and smoke a little with George and some of his friends. We knew a lot of the same people since we both grew up in Milford and went to the same high school. It was during one of these hangouts that I realized that George and his dad rented one of the rooms in their house to this kid, Jay, who I grew up with as well.

Jay came home from work just as we were rolling up a joint. We were waiting on a few other people to come over as well, but Jay said he'd join us after taking a shower. So, Jay goes into the shower and the other people come by. One of them I knew very well, as he was my old training partner on the wrestling team, a kid named Elijah. I had never seen the other one before in my life, but he seemed nice enough I guess.

We were hanging out, smoking a little, and making chit-chat when Jay comes out of his room after getting dressed. He locks eyes with Elijah's friend and becomes rage incarnate. He flies across the room and starts swinging at him like a maniac. A stream of curse words came flowing from his mouth and George leaped from his seat and restrained Jay, screaming "not in my house, not in my house". I jumped from my spot as well because I had no idea what was happening and did not want to be sitting down if trouble somehow managed to come my way. Elijah's friend was standing now trying to get a piece, so George and Elijah broke them up again. Jay wriggled out of George's grip but I got in front of him and kept him from attacking Elijah's friend while he screamed and cursed him out. George told Elijah to get that kid out of there and they left.

Jay went into his room. George apologized profusely to me and his other friend who sat and watched the whole thing while he bogarted the joint for himself. After a few minutes, Jay came out still looking riled up. George asked him what that was all about and Jay told us that kid ratted out a couple of his friends who were pushing weight and got them sent to jail. I could understand why the sight of such a person would put Jay into such a frenzy.

Thankfully, most of the time I spent at George's house was not nearly as exciting. We mostly just talked about work with the occasional update about George's on-again-off-again relationship. George was a nervous guy, especially for someone who went to prison. Or perhaps he was nervous *because* of the time he spent inside. Either way, he was always looking for advice and affirmations. I didn't mind helping him out. Relationships are hard and it's always good to have a sympathetic ear.

The grind of making calls was actually paying off. Not long after George secured our first meeting with a career center staff member, I got a few meetings on the hook as well, including one at my alma mater. It was nice because with each meeting we set we would get a small incentive payment of ten bucks. It wasn't much, but it was something. Christina assured us that we would get more as time went on and the company had actual funds at its disposal.

We drove up to Boston to meet with the career center staff. It was clear sunny skies on the drive up, but as we got closer clouds started rolling in. By the time we got to campus it was pissing rain and the closest parking lot to the office we were meeting in was about a block away as the crow flies. I had one medium-sized umbrella that Christina, George, and I had to share. We crowded underneath it, but it did little to keep us dry in the downpour. My only pair of nice shoes were filling with water as we hurried to our meeting.

They brought us in and we looked like a bunch of drowned rats. Not long after, they brought us to a conference room where we waited and tried to dry out. The leather portfolio that I took notes in was wet but somehow not ruined. Eventually, the career services person came in. Christina looked at me to start the meeting since this was my connection. I was taken a little off-guard by the rain but jumped into the pitch we had talked about on the two and half hour drive up. I gave a brief overview of the company and Christina took over.

She swatted down every question posed with ease. This was because most of the answers she was giving were complete bullshit. I remember being dumbfounded as lies of omission or outright falsehoods flowed from Christina's mouth. One thing in particular that stands out in my memory was the career services person asking how we scheduled our interview experts. Christina said that we use a model similar to Uber's, where interviewers can pick and choose when they want to interview at their leisure. Of course, this was a lie. We didn't have the technological infrastructure in place to make that possible, nor did we have nearly enough interviewers on hand to meet such a demand, nor did we have any customers to speak of. I don't know if this was something that Christina and Brett had discussed on their own, but as far as I knew this was a complete fabrication.

Eventually, the career services person leveled with us. They had no interest in the product at all and only took the meeting because I was an alumnus. Of course, we were disappointed by the response, but Christina decided to make lemonade and took the opportunity to get some insight into the needs and demands of a career services department. We ended up talking for another half hour or so, learning about how these people think and what they need, so it wasn't a total loss.

After our meeting, we went and got some food at one of my favorite burger places in Boston and licked our wounds. The rain had mostly cleared up, so we walked over to the restaurant. It was nice to be back in Boston, but also kind of bittersweet. We ate and had a couple of beers. Christina didn't seem fazed by the rejection. We talked a little and George started to express dissatisfaction with his relationship with his girlfriend, as was tradition whenever we spent more than a half-hour together. Christina and I had just about enough of it and told him flat out that he needed to end things with her. George told us that he knew, but it was hard because he cared about her. We took turns trying to explain to him that while we believed that he cared about her, it was clear that this relationship was a strain on him and was stealing energy from him that could be better spent elsewhere. If only we had known how true those words would be for all of us.

Chapter XII

We had a few more meetings and calls, but nothing was materializing. Christina was not rattled. After all, this was a brand-new business. Brett, on the other hand, was becoming more worried by the day. He started to get on our case about the number of hours we were logging and how we were treating him like our personal ATM. Considering he was paying us 10 bucks an hour to build his company and hadn't even gotten us our contracts that sealed the deal on our equity, I found this to be a particularly unreasonable accusation.

His behavior was becoming more erratic. One day I went to meet him at his house in the sunporch office with George. He was twitchy and wouldn't stop talking. At first, I thought he was on coke and I asked him if he was feeling okay. He looked awful. He told me that he'd been up all night doing Adderall and trying to figure out a way to "save the company". He asked us how the sales calls were going and I told him that we'd had a few meetings on the books but nothing substantial yet. Brett was not pleased with that answer and asked us how we were selling the company, clearly convinced that the reason we weren't closing deals was because of our approach. George looked at me for help and I shrugged and told him that we were following Christina's training and getting meetings but having some trouble sealing the deal.

Brett asked us who we had been calling, his suspicions turning to us screwing off on the job instead of making calls. I told him we were focusing on Connecticut. He asked to see our spreadsheet and notes, so George pulled it up on his computer. After looking over George's shoulder while he scrolled through the notes verifying we had, in fact, made calls and spoken with people. Brett then demanded that George make a call right there in front of him. I didn't know what to say. Brett was on a tear and I didn't think I'd be able to talk him down. George reluctantly put his headphones in and dialed one of the names on the list. I hoped that nobody would pick up. George was pretty good on the phone, but generally not great under duress. Brett's glassy-eyed leering was definitely enough to put him off his game. The phone kept ringing.

Unfortunately, someone answered. George said hello and started into his pitch the way that Christina had taught us. It seemed to be going well, or at least not horribly. Then Brett reached over and plucked one of the headphones from George's ear and put it in his own, crowding in to keep the cord from stretching. I couldn't believe it. George couldn't either. Brett motioned for George to keep talking despite his obvious breach of decency and privacy. I couldn't watch. I pretended I had to go to the bathroom and went downstairs to avoid watching a trainwreck unfold before my eyes.

When I came back upstairs, George was off the phone looking quite unhappy. Brett said that the call went okay when I asked. He added that we needed to figure out a way to get some more money in and that he was going to have to find some more investors. He tacked on a joke that he was going to have to go to the casino to try to win some money for us. In retrospect, I realize that this is not a sign of a healthy company and that I was very much on a sinking ship. Even at the time, this gave me some pause, but Christina's confidence and guidance were enough to buoy my doubts about Brett.

Chapter XIII

My first real bite came when I called a community college in Hartford. A woman answered and was excited to speak with me about how our company could support her. Her name was Melissa. She seemed quite unhappy with how she was being treated and I guess just needed a sympathetic ear because we talked for about a half-hour before I set an in-person meeting with her and Christina. Though I had set some meetings up to that point, this was the first one that I felt like could lead somewhere. It was a good feeling and almost made up for the fact that I was getting paid peanuts and hemorrhaging money.

The tutoring was just barely paying the rent. I needed some more cash to keep me going, as I had other expenses. Coincidentally, Jason and I were getting to be pretty good friends. Outside of his cool, aloof exterior was a good dude who was smart and had a dark sense of humor. He was living with his grandmother after moving back from California and I would occasionally go to his house and chill and smoke weed with him. One time I went over there when I was running low and I asked him if he had a plug. He told me that he did and said he could set me up if I wanted, as he was good friends with his dealer and could get me a great price. I asked him how great and when he told me how much an ounce was, I nearly fell out of my chair. I immediately realized that I could make a little bit of scratch selling some weed to the myriad stoners I knew in the area at the rates he was giving me, so I had him pick me up a quarter-pound and I was off to the races.

Like most stoners, I was no stranger to flipping a bag here or there when people asked for a little help. It's kind of an unspoken rule among pot smokers to sell a gram out of your bag if a friend asks you for it, similar to how there's an unspoken rule among cigarette smokers to give someone a loosey if they ask for one. This was a little different for me, though. I had never sold weed before because I needed the money. It was always either because I was helping out a friend or because I wanted to smoke for free.

I wasn't the only one flipping bags to make ends meet either. Though he never explicitly told me he was doing so, I think Jason was also selling bags. Though he appeared to prefer to deal in the much more lucrative market of oils and concentrates, something I never had much interest in. I remember one time we were at Phil's house and George, Christina, and I were talking in the living room about an upcoming meeting. Jason was in his usual place working on his computer. A car pulled up in front of the house and Jason's phone rang. He got up, ran outside, stuck his head in the car window for a few minutes, then hustled back in. Nobody seemed to notice, or at least nobody said anything about it. But I remember thinking that it was an extremely ballsy move to do a drug deal in front of your job.

Brett and Phil were also getting increasingly concerned about the company coffers. They were getting so worried that they were starting to seek out angel investors for funding. And what they quickly found was that serious investors want to invest in serious companies. So that meant we needed to put together a bunch of materials to show that we were serious. We needed to write an executive statement and a proper business plan that included some solid market research.

Christina was surprised and annoyed that Brett and Phil hadn't already had these materials put together. She told me privately later on that when they first brought her aboard the company, Brett had told her that he had a business plan and had done market research and she felt that he had pulled a bait and switch with this lie. But we were already stuck in this, so we got to work on writing something. It was a miserable slog that took several days to finalize. One reason why things took so long was that Brett and Christina would keep butting heads. Brett would propose something, Christina would either refine it or explain why it's not a good idea, and Brett would get all huffy and try to fall back on his experience running his landscaping company. What Brett never seemed to fully grasp was that we weren't trying to be like a landscaping company, we were trying to be like one of the slick Fortune 500 companies that Christina used to work for. Of course, this was Brett's vision as well, but he failed to see that our company needed to function like one to make that vision a reality.

It was clear Brett felt threatened by Christina's dazzling level of confidence and knowledge. Once, we went out to get lunch together just the two of us at Café Atlantique and Brett asked me, without a shred of irony or humor, if I thought he was smart. Talk about a loaded question. I chewed my food thoughtfully and tried to formulate an answer that would disarm this bomb he had presented me with.

I swallowed and told him that I thought there were many different types of intelligence and that, like everyone else, he was smart in some ways and less smart in others. I didn't lie to Brett because it was true that he had a way with people, but I also omitted my thought that in many other ways, particularly the ways that were essential to the functioning and future success of our business, I thought Brett was a spectacular dumbass. Of course, I wouldn't tell him that even though he seemed to be asking for my honest opinion. I knew Brett well enough to know that when he felt threatened or that his ego had been bruised, he lashed out. And I had still not gotten my contract locking in my chunk of the company Brett had promised me, so I didn't feel like putting everything I had done and sacrificed on the line for a moment of brutal honesty.

Thankfully, he seemed pretty satisfied with my answer and nodded his head as though he was genuinely going to reflect on my remarks. We talked a little more and the subject of money came up. Brett asked me how things were going and this time I could not spare him the truth. I told him that money was getting tight and that I was starting to struggle. Brett said he knew the feeling and that the company was also getting tight on money. I tried to restrain my anger as much as possible when I pointed out to him that while he had put a lot of his own money on the line, he was still making money with his landscaping company and wasn't worrying about how he was going to make his rent this month. Brett shrugged and said that if I wanted to, I could pull weeds for him at ten bucks an hour to make some extra cash. All I could do is give a contemptuous little laugh and shake my head and tell him that I didn't think it would come to that.

    I find this exchange exemplary of Brett's entire approach to management. Brett was not shy about asking the people working for him for just about anything. But he was never interested in any kind of reciprocation. He was always about getting the most he possibly could for the lowest possible price. And even when he thought he was being generous or kind, all he managed to do was be even more insulting and exploitative. I genuinely think that Brett believed his offer to let me pull weeds for him at minimum wage was helpful and kind. I don't think he realized how it could be considered insulting or wrong to pay someone such a small amount of money for a job that generated huge profits for him. I was particularly insulted because Brett knew I had very profitable skills beyond my ability to pull weeds and he was purposefully ignoring them. I have nothing against people who pull weeds for a living. It is work that is necessary that they should be paid a living wage for. Especially when the honest work that weed pullers do makes guys like Brett wealthy.

Chapter XIV

When we weren't making our calls or building out the database in neighboring states, we were always looking for ways to get our company's name out there. Often, this meant leveraging our personal relationships. George had a connection with a community center in New Haven that wanted to run a workshop on preparing for job interviews for some local teenagers. So, we set up an event to teach these kids interview skills even though none of us except for Phil and Christina had much experience teaching people these skills. This also meant that we had to create an itinerary for the event.

We all got together and put together some interview tips and mock interview questions to use on the day. After that, we created an evaluation system to judge how well students did and to communicate what they could improve on. I don't remember if it was our connection or if it was through someone else at the community center, but there was also a keynote speaker on the bill. She was a woman named Denise who had worked at the White House with several different administrations. Truly, her list of accomplishments was so impressive that it made me wonder if we were out of our league.

On the day of the event, Brett, George, Jason, Phil, and I all went to the community center. Christina for whatever reason was unavailable to join us. We were all dressed up in suits and ties and were taken into a conference room while the staff was getting everything ready. Denise was sitting in there with a bottle of water looking at her phone. We said hello and all sat down trying to project dignity. Even Brett's unflappable confidence was slipping. Denise was weirdly spacey. At first, I thought she might've been on benzos or some kind of medication. She would talk in this quiet little voice and nod when someone said something, but it didn't seem like she was really listening or that the words were sinking in. Maybe she just thought we were boring and didn't want to talk to us. After all, she was used to rubbing elbows with presidents and other powerful people.

    Eventually, the time came for us to do our little song and dance. We all went down into a gymnasium where all the kids were waiting at these tables they set up for the event. George got out in front and started with a little introduction. Then Brett got out, after some prodding from Phil and me, and said a few words to the kids though he was quite reluctant and was unprepared. Jason filmed his speech, always cognizant of our social media presence. We then broke up into little groups and ran our practice interviews. It wasn't anything I hadn't done before. After all, I was still tutoring kids not far from where we were in New Haven, so I treated the entire experience as an extension of that. Once that portion was done, Denise got up and spoke. I don't know where that dazed woman in the conference room went. Denise's voice boomed as she gave her speech, rousing the kids from their inattention with a call and response. She talked about her journey to success and then moved on to their futures and about how important it was to build skills today to be successful tomorrow. Honestly, the content of the speech was nothing new or different from the standard motivational fare. It was her energy that brought it to life and filled that gym with a real sense of potential and possibility. We were in disbelief. I remember being very relieved that Brett did not have to speak after Denise.

    When Christina saw the video of Brett speaking, she was not happy. The first thing she asked was why Brett was holding a water bottle. The entire time he was speaking to these kids, he was holding a plastic water bottle so tight it looked like the lid was going to pop off. None of us thought to take it away from him before he got out in front of them. In truth, I think it helped him deal with the performance anxiety. Christina was also not happy with the actual content of his speech, which was meandering and unrehearsed. We all agreed that the next time we held an event, Brett would have to have something prepared and be coached on how to hold himself if he was going to speak.

Chapter XV

Events were becoming more commonplace, though thankfully Brett did not have any more speaking engagements. My community college account was leading someplace. Melissa was very enthusiastic about our product and wanted to give us a chance to demonstrate to the higher-ups at her school the potential value of what we were doing. So, I worked with her to create a virtual job interview fair where students could come and sample our services and get some free job interview training. It was basically a dry run for implementing our program at a school, something we had never done before despite what we told people in our sales meetings.

This meant that we had to make a ton of preparations. We needed to come up with interview questions, scorecards, and a framework for the general structure of the event. Moreover, we did not have enough interview experts on our staff, which meant that George, Jason, Brett, Christina, and I all had to conduct interviews with students as well. In preparation for this event, we all sat around Phil's dining room table and took turns pretending to be interviewers and students.

It was fun because we encouraged one another to be difficult or to otherwise make common mistakes interviewers made. I remember being particularly amused by Phil's students, who would focus on one hobby and be completely unable to talk about anything else. I think I found it so funny because I had never really seen Phil commit to a joke like that before and it took me by surprise. Christina would stop us and give feedback if things were going south, but for the most part, everyone seemed to have a good idea of what to do. We put together a scorecard to be completed and then emailed to the students, which would also provide proof to the staff and administration that we were providing valuable feedback. Everything was coming together.

The night before the event, I was at Phil's house helping

George and Jason and Phil figure out where everyone was going to work. It was a challenge because there wasn't much room and we needed to make sure that there wasn't any ambient noise from the other calls in addition to making sure that the camera angle didn't betray the fact that we were conducting these interviews from inside someone's house and not in a world-class cutting edge facility that we told people existed. So, it was a tedious evening of making test video calls, rearranging furniture, adjusting lights, tacking up sheets, and taping down marks on the floor. But we got it done and felt pretty good about running our event the next day.

  I don't remember what the plan was exactly. I think Brett was supposed to accompany me to the event so that he could introduce himself to the career services staff and get a little facetime with the president of the school, who was going to come and check out our event for himself. What I do remember clearly is having to go to the event alone, disregarding the original plan to have someone with me to help set up and make sure everything ran smoothly. I wore my one good suit, which was navy blue and made of wool and was carrying a box of materials for the students and staff.

  I met with Melissa in her office and she was thrilled as usual to see me. There were a bunch of students waiting in line to get their interviews going and she informed me that a few members of her department were able to interview. She was disappointed to find that Brett was unable to join me, but I made up some excuse to explain his absence. We got the event rolling.

  I distributed the sample questions and scorecards to the interviewers that were waiting for me. Melissa then showed me to my workstation in a computer lab where I would be conducting my own video interviews. I had about fifteen minutes to collect myself before the event started. I was anxious, which was normal for me. In the moments leading up to a performance, especially one in an event I'm running, I get hit with anxiety bordering on full mania. My stomach churns and I feel sick but in an amorphous sort of way. I usually can't eat or even really maintain any kind of meaningful conversation until I've gotten my performance over with. Luckily, I didn't have to wait long to get this show on the road. After a few minutes of failing to meditate, my computer informed me that someone was attempting a video call.

As I began conducting my first interview with the student on the other end, I realized that I had absolutely nothing to be nervous about. In my panicked worrying, I had forgotten about the power dynamic of a job interview. This is to say that being the person conducting the interview and evaluating the student, I had all the power. Moreover, these students made it clear very early on that they were completely clueless about how to behave in an interview, so I didn't exactly have to work hard to impress them or to show them how knowledgeable I was.

The interviews followed a pattern where students would connect, I would welcome them and tell them not to be nervous and to treat this conversation like a real job interview, then jump right into the standard job interview questions. After picking a few random ones off my list and adding in some of my own that the flow of conversation brought on organically, I would end the interview by inviting students to ask me any questions about the pretend job or company in question. This is where most of the students would screw up. They were all so concerned about their answers, that they forgot to consider the fact a job interview is ultimately a two-way street. So, I ended up getting some amusing responses to that last question. Most notably, one student asked me why I have such dark circles around my eyes, which are an extremely prominent feature of my face. It doesn't matter how much rest I get or how much I moisturize, they're a permanent fixture. Both of my parents and both of my sisters have them as well. I've long since come to embrace them as part of what makes my face unique. Still, it's quite rude to point like that out something to someone you've just met, let alone during a job interview. I wasn't offended, mostly shocked that he had asked that question and not… anything else. Sometimes I wonder what that kid is doing these days.

After all my questions were answered and the student logged off, I'd complete my scorecard and put it in the folder to give to Melissa, who would see to it that each student would get the feedback. I couldn't say how many interviews I did that day. Once the event got started, it was a blur. But at the end of the day,

Melissa was happy. Ecstatic even. She wanted me to meet with the president of the university.

I don't know what I was expecting. Someone taller, probably. The president was a small elderly Indian man with a head of thick white hair. He had a grandfatherly smile when he shook my hand and told me how impressed he was with how our event went. I thanked him for the opportunity to show him how our product works and asked him if he would like to learn about what we do at length. Christine's training had done me well. I had gotten very good at judging when to press and when to pull back on a client. He smiled and said that he would enjoy that, but his schedule is very tight so it would have to be some time far in the future. He gave me his business card as well as one belonging to his executive assistant and instructed me to set up a meeting through them. I assured him that I would and we parted ways.

I couldn't believe it. I closed my hands around the president's business card and was overcome with a wild sense of optimism. Things were really happening. The president of a university wanted to sit down and talk about our product because of me. This was the last step before finally closing a deal. And what's more, was that it was my deal, and I was the one who had done most of the legwork. I packed up and drove home feeling like the whole world was within my reach.

Chapter XVI

Not long after this event, Brett finally got us our equity contracts. I remember when he handed me the paper, slipping it into my hands in Phil's hallway like it was a drug deal. He spoke in a low voice when he told me that this was my contract like he didn't want anyone else to hear. I should have taken this as a red flag considering Brett was acting like he was doing something wrong, but I was so excited to get the contract that I didn't think twice about his behavior at the time. My excitement evaporated as I read the sheet.

This contract was a total piece of shit. I was in disbelief as to how Brett could possibly think I would ever sign such a one-sided and exploitative agreement. It locked me in as an independent contractor instead of a proper employee with all the legal responsibilities that relationship affords. There was nothing about increasing my wages, which were at the time at the state minimum wage of $10/hour. There was nothing about getting a commission on any deals I help bring in. There was the same piddly $10 commission on each meeting set, paid a month after a meeting would take place, giving Brett the opportunity to withhold payment if the meeting gets canceled, and a modest bonus of $50 for setting 10 meetings in a week. But most insulting of all was I would only be able to access my equity if I was still employed with the company after a 3-year vesting period for one percent of the company. One percent. Of the company whose mission statement I wrote. I was furious.

Despite my rage, I knew better than to just storm in guns blazing and tell Brett where to go. After all, I still wanted some equity in the company. Especially now that we had a meeting with the president of a school on our books in the distant future. My pride was telling me to go, but my greed urged me to stay. Once again, my greed won out and I devised a plan.

There was no way I was going to sign the contract as it was written. I started by talking to George to see if he was given the same offer as me. I knew that George had put some of his own money in as an investment, so I wasn't sure if he was given the same amount of equity. As it turns out, Brett had given George the same contract as me. I asked him if he was satisfied with what Brett was trying to get us to sign and George confessed that he had reservations. I told George that I was going to make a bunch of amendments to mine. He asked me if I wouldn't mind sharing my proposed amendments with him, as he thought it would be a good idea if we put up a unified front. I agreed and set to work slicing up our contracts like a surgeon with a scalpel.

It took a few days for me to work up the nerve to send my amendments over to Brett. I remember sitting in George's kitchen going through all the changes with him one last time before we both finally attached our contracts to an email and hit send. I felt like I was going to puke and half expected my phone to immediately start buzzing with a furious Brett on the other line. I remembered the last time I asked Brett for what I felt I deserved and how badly it had gone and was terrified that it would happen again with much higher stakes. Of course, what I didn't realize at the time was that Brett had no leverage in this situation. It wasn't like he could have offered me a worse contract. The only thing he could have done was take the offer off the table immediately, but I think he was sharp enough to realize that one of the only things keeping me around was the chance of getting a piece of the company, which he would continually say could be worth hundreds of thousands of dollars. Looking back, I wish I had pressed harder at the negotiating table. But, then again, I was going broke and at the time did not feel like rolling the dice with a job that I felt had potential for success, even if that potential was waning.

After a few days, I stopped flinching every time my phone rang. After a few weeks, I started wondering if Brett had gotten my email. When Brett urged us that it was paramount for us to sign our contracts and return them to him as quickly as possible, I asked him if he had gotten my email about my amendments to the contract. He said that he had been so busy that he hadn't had the chance to look at them yet, but he'd get to it as soon as he could. And that was the last I had heard of it for a while.

I couldn't help but scoff when Brett would talk about how busy he was running two companies and trying to wrangle funding for our start-up and also have a social life with his new girlfriend. This was because I had gotten an inside scoop on some of Brett's extracurricular activities. By chance, I met a day laborer at Brett's house one day who called himself Uncle Derek that would occasionally do some odd jobs for Brett. Uncle Derek mentioned needing a hookup for weed, so I started selling him bags. I would stop at his house and we'd make chit chat. It turned out that Uncle Derek was a massive gossip and would tell me all about what Brett was up to. He told me that Brett was going up to the casino almost every weekend and blasting lines of Adderall and blow to stay up all night gambling. So, when Brett would complain about being so tired from all the work he was doing, I'd roll my eyes because I knew what was really going on.

Chapter XVII

While our pay was dismal, there was somehow room in the budget for marketing. Brett shelled out some money on a billboard advertising our company for reasons that to this day remain unclear to me. I don't think I've ever seen a business advertised on a billboard and was convinced that I needed that product or service, except for the billboards featuring close-up pictures of food. Considering when I usually see a billboard it's only for a few seconds as I'm whipping by at 80 miles per hour, it seemed like a waste of money for Brett to pay for one. I think the billboard was more than anything else Brett playing Big Company, or rather what he thought big companies did.

Our marketing efforts didn't stop there either. While I'm not sure about the specifics, I'm certain Brett was also pumping money into our social media ad budget. Brett was also very keen on putting together a commercial to advertise our "Gift a Grad" program. The idea behind this was that nervous relatives would give the people graduating college the gift of some job interview training instead of the boring old gift of cash in a card. So, we outlined an ad and brought in a kid we had gone to high school with named Steve who was running his own freelance film production company.

George worked with Steve as a de facto producer wrangling actors, storyboarding scenes, and supervising shoots, while also serving as a walk-on actor. I wrote the voice-over and recorded myself performing it. It all came together more or less without a hitch. Once we got a final cut of the commercial together after about 2 weeks of work, we gathered everyone around Phil's kitchen table and showed them.

Christina was not pleased. Immediately, she pointed out that there were only white people in the video and very few women. It was a sharp call on her part. She insisted that we were going to have to shoot more scenes to include more diversity. Brett pushed back a little when she first started, complaining about the additional cost and editing time, but Christina did not relent and the rest of us agreed with her. So, it was back to work. We eventually did get the project finished and it was much stronger with Christina's added scenes.

After we launched the commercial with Christina's blessing, I remember going to George's house to celebrate a little. It was just the two of us in his living room smoking weed and watching some TV, trying to avoid talking about work even though it was one of the only things we had in common that we could discuss at length. George started complaining about money and how broke he was. I was making good money selling weed and offered to set George up with a bit to make a little side cash for himself. He took me up on the offer immediately and I agreed to front him an ounce. We hung out a little longer then George's phone started ringing. It was his girlfriend. After a brief exchange, George hung up the phone, looked over at me nervously, and told me that she was coming over now.

A pregnant pause hung between us. It seemed like he was expecting me to say something or to take a cue to leave. Being quite high, I was very agreeable and out of it, so I just shrugged and told him that was fine and that I wouldn't mind meeting her and chilling with her. This did not seem to help George's nervousness but, ever the people pleaser, he did not ask me to leave.

Not long after, George's girlfriend showed up. At least, I think she did. A humanoid blur came through the front door and immediately marched into George's room, giving me just enough time to say hello before she disappeared. George apologized and went into the other room to talk to her, leaving me alone to play with his dog. After a few minutes, George came back and apologized for her. I told him that there wasn't anything to apologize for and we continued chilling. Then his phone began buzzing with incoming texts from his girlfriend. She wanted him to bring her the grinder and weed that we had out here. I laughed in disbelief. I didn't know who to feel sorrier for: this girl who felt that this was an appropriate way to act, or for George who was indulging her. I told George not to bring her the stuff and that if she wanted it, she could come out and get it like an adult.

George hesitated and ultimately agreed with me. His phone continued to blow up with texts until finally she came out and in a huff snatched up the gear she wanted and stomped off. As she was leaving, I asked her if I smelled and if that was why she didn't want to sit with us. It was a little immature and dickish of me, but I was so taken aback by how rude this girl was that I could not just let such ridiculous behavior slide. In hindsight, I recognize that there could have been any number of reasons why she would have behaved in such a way, but I think it was the combination of her stalwart commitment to being an asshole, George's lack of explanation for such behavior, and the myriad stories that George had told me about her, that kept me from giving her much sympathy or compassion.

George's phone started ringing. She was calling him and she did not seem happy on the other end. I laughed and shook my head and got up, taking my cue to leave. I felt a little bad because I probably put George in the doghouse. He was apologetic as he walked me to the door and told me that she wasn't usually like that. I shrugged and told him it was fine and was on my way. In truth, it was such a bizarre exchange that I was more amused than annoyed.

Chapter XVIII

Things were getting tense in Phil's house. Brett and Christina would butt heads more frequently. Apparently, Brett had asked Christina if she wanted to invest any of her own money to help float the company. Considering she had been working without any kind of wage for months, I found that to be a particularly bold request that only a guy like Brett would even think of making. Once she declined, he followed up by asking if she knew anyone that she could shakedown for potential investment opportunities. I should note that Brett had the tact and shame to make these requests in private, but Christina and I were good friends at this point and she would later relate these stories to me after the fact.

We were still taking meetings and making calls, but there was an air of desperation creeping upon us. Money was getting tighter and Brett was becoming a bigger liability. His problem was that he thought he was far smarter than he was. I don't think it ever occurred to him that other people could see through him.

For example, once Brett tried to pull one over on a career services person at one of the many colleges we were reaching out to. Brett got the bright idea to pretend to be a student and called this person looking for information on mock interviews, I guess to make it seem like there was a demand for the services we were offering. Considering Brett had just gotten through emailing this person as well, they caught on to what he was trying to do and got a nasty email calling out his duplicity and his unprofessionalism and more or less said that not only would they not be doing business with us, but also that we've made an enemy for life. Christina was furious, of course. He had burned a bridge for no reason and made us look like a gaggle of assholes.

But things weren't all bad. There were a couple of deals on the line that could easily solve all our troubles. I had set an appointment with that community college president, which would be a small but much-needed win if we closed the deal. George, on the other hand, had a whale on the line that he was in the process of reeling in inch by inch. The career services rep for one of the biggest colleges in Pennsylvania was interested in our product, which would change everything if we landed the deal. This was a school that had tens of thousands of students and even just interviews for a fraction of them would be a life-changing boon.

Through happenstance, we also had the opportunity to get publicity and face time with some of the head honchos in the Connecticut state government. There was an event at the state capitol building celebrating the city of Milford and the Mayor asked me if I wanted to attend and read a poem as Poet Laureate and set up a table to sell books or promote myself. Since I didn't have any books at the time to sell, I asked if it would be okay to give my spot to our startup to promote our services. They graciously agreed.

In the end, we got to set up a table alongside some massive multibillion-dollar global corporations headquartered in lil ol' Milford, Connecticut, including one of the largest manufacturers of razors and probably the most famous sandwich franchise on the planet. I got up and read a poem for everyone about how great Milford is, got some light applause, and then sat around with Christina, George, and Jason. A few people came up and spoke with us, mostly to say hi to me and commend me on my poem, but some people were genuinely curious about what we did. For the most part, I was pretty bored and in retrospect wish that I hadn't given up my spot for the start-up. It wasn't that we were unwelcome or anyone was rude or had a problem with us being there, it was just that it was kind of a waste of a day and I probably would have had more fun if I just hobnobbed and chitchatted instead of manning a table.

Chapter XIX

The money problems were becoming impossible to ignore and Brett was becoming increasingly desperate for cash. I'm not sure exactly how it happened, I think it was possibly one of Jason's connections, but we somehow managed to get in contact with a person who was part of the casting team of an immensely popular reality TV show. It was a Hail Marry pass for funding, but it was the only card that we had left.

Now, I never watched this show, though I was familiar with the concept. People would go on TV to pitch their businesses and the billionaire mogul judges would ask questions and then decide whether or not they want to invest based on the answers. As it turns out, there's an incredibly long vetting process before a contestant steps foot on set. First, we needed to do a phone interview, which Brett somehow managed to not screw up, likely because Christina was also on the call and he wisely let her do most of the talking.

The next step was to film a pitch both to show that we had our shit together enough to produce a decent video and that we looked good enough on camera to be put on national television. We drafted up a short script where Brett, Phil, and Christina would pitch the company with as much personality and enthusiasm as they could muster and filmed it over two days, mostly on Brett's phone with Jason working the camera.

Since then, I've filmed quite a few things and know far more about creating a high-quality production on a non-existent budget. I think we did the best we could with our knowledge and budget at the time, but in many ways, we fell short. We simply did not have the expertise, equipment, or funds to make a good video.

On the first day of shooting, we were by the duck pond in downtown Milford, which was an iconic spot that we thought would give the producers a taste of our local character. Jason manned the camera. I was the de facto director and script supervisor shouting orders between takes and cutting people off when they got their lines or delivery wrong. Phil once again surprised me with his energy and enthusiasm as a performer. He kept doing this bit where he called himself a rhino, itself a callback to an exercise we did together where we tried to describe ourselves as animals. He chewed on the scenery by basically growling his line, which I found very funny and kept encouraging him to do. Christina had a saccharine peppiness that did a good job of counterbalancing Phil's gruff affected masculinity. Brett had the most trouble with organically delivering his lines and needed the most coaching, though this was something I had expected since he was not a skilled public speaker. We probably ran through 20 takes that afternoon before the sun started to set and we had to call it a day because the change in light was messing up our shot. I don't know if any of the footage was usable because even though Phil and Christina were better performers than Brett, they both started off the shoot tense and tentative as well.

With the deadline to get our materials to the producers rapidly approaching, Brett loosened his grip on his wallet enough to put up Christina in a hotel for the night so that we can continue filming the next day. Having learned our lesson from the previous day, we elected to shoot indoors, taking advantage of the hotel's empty meeting room. All three of them were quick learners and took some of the instructions I had given them to heart. Even Brett gave a much better performance. We knocked out the shoot in about half a day and Jason took all the footage to cut it together into a 10-minute video.

We gave it our best shot, but in the end, the show decided to go in a different direction. I think part of the reason why they passed on having us on the show was the fact that most companies featured do some kind of demonstration or at least have a physical product to show off, whereas our business was service-based and difficult to demonstrate in a way that would be interesting for television audiences. The producers did say that they thought the idea had merit and that perhaps further down the line they'd change their position and give us a spot on the show, which was encouraging, if also a little bittersweet for us.

We had missed, but we weren't down and out yet. There was still George's big Pennsylvania deal that was giving us all enough hope and motivation to keep scooping buckets of water out of the sinking ship. Though in private, Christina and Jason both expressed their doubts about the future of the company. I knew that if they bailed, it was over. The whole thing would be dead in the water. This is not meant to be a slight against Phil or George, who were also doing important work, but Christina and Jason were so skilled and competent at their respective roles that their departure would be a killing blow, particularly if Christina left, as Brett had already proved countless times that he did not have the skills or experience needed to bring this company to where he wanted it to go.

Chapter XX

Spring semesters all over the country were wrapping up, which meant that administrators would be reviewing their budgets for the following school year. We knew that now was the time to try to seal some deals. By luck, there was a conference for college and university administrators taking place and our contact from Pennsylvania would be in attendance. Brett and Christina agreed that it would be best for them to meet her there and try to close this deal, as well as get some face time with other college admins. I did not attend and enjoyed a relatively quiet week in Phil's kitchen with George making calls.

When they returned, Christina told me that she never wanted to travel with Brett again. Her biggest complaint, unsurprisingly, was that he did not have his shit together when traveling and they had to rush to get everywhere they went. I could see how this would be particularly annoying to Christina, who was a veteran traveler for both business and pleasure and likely had a whole system that Brett rendered useless. In a team meeting after their return, they told us that they spent half the conference pouring drinks down this lady's throat and schmoozing her as best as they could. Christina sounded confident that this deal would come through.

Privately, however, Christina confided to me that the company was dead in the water. Brett was not the person to lead the company to any sort of material success. I don't know what happened between them at the conference, but I imagine there was some serious discussion about the future of the company where they could not come to an agreement. She told me that she was going to be leaving the company and that she'd try to hook George and me up with some other job if and when she could. I told her that if she was leaving then I was also going to leave, since I had no patience for Brett's dumbfuckery at this point, especially considering the abysmal contract he was offering me that he had completely ignored my amendments on.

I wasn't sure how the others were going to take the news. Primarily Brett. He was volatile on his best day and with all the Adderall and stress of burning through most of our money, he was even worse. I was there when Christina sat down and told Phil and Brett that she was going to have to move on, specifically saying that she needed money. They took it shockingly well. They wished her the best of luck in all her future endeavors, each hugged her, and thanked her for all her help. Before she left, she made sure to say goodbye to me and then gave me three envelopes: one was a letter for me and the other two were for George and Jason. And then she was gone.

The team meeting the following day had a sense of battered and affected optimism. Everyone knew that losing Christina was a crippling blow. What's more, was that my meeting with the president was coming up and we had just lost our greatest asset. Part of me wanted to immediately follow through on what I told Christina: that if she was gone, then so was I. But I knew that the right thing to do was to see this meeting through and hope this one last attempt at locking in some revenue worked. Not just for the company's sake, either. I was dead broke and the tutoring work was starting to dry up as the students took their final exams. I promised myself to make a final decision after this meeting with the president.

I remember seeing George at his new apartment in the days leading up to this meeting. We lamented Christina's departure and cursed Brett for both his incompetence and greed. George, being his right-hand man for all of Brett's business endeavors, quietly informed me that he knew that Brett had a bank account full of cash that he never touched, a kind of locked-down savings. This, of course, made me furious. After all, I wasn't even making enough money to survive and the equity I was being offered was absolute dogshit. I had neglected all my other clients and put all my eggs in Brett's basket. It was a colossal fuck up, but part of me still wanted to limp on and see if I could work something better out. I was hoping to either negotiate with Brett for a better contract or seal a deal and get a cut of the revenue. It was a notion fueled by delusion, pride, and greed.

The day of the meeting arrived. I put on my one good suit, mentally preparing myself to lead the meeting. Brett would be backing me up instead of Christina, but I was ready to take the reins on this one since I had already built up a relationship with the school and the president. It was an hour ride up to the school and Brett had agreed to drive, so we both piled into the cluttered cab of his truck.

We talked about our game plan and how we would try to sell the company to this president. Though, in a typical Brett fashion, he changed the subject whenever something else popped into his head. At one point, he mentioned that I had still not signed and submitted my contract to him and that I needed to do that as soon as possible. Confused, I asked Brett if he looked at the proposed amendments I had made to the contract. He said that he was too busy and hadn't gotten a chance even though it had been two months since he had given me the contract. He then, defensively, asked what I even wanted to change in the first place. At this point, I was incredulous and unable to control my outrage. I told Brett that the contract he had given me was an insult and that I would never sign it, specifically citing the pitiful one percent ownership of the company and the fact there was nothing written in there about raising my wages. Brett countered by grumbling that we should drop the subject right now since we had a very important meeting coming up, that he was driving, and that he wanted to punch me in the face.

At the time, I was so angry and fired up that I remembered thinking, even with our stark difference in size, that Brett should go right ahead and try punching me in the face, that it wouldn't change how I felt about the contract at all. It was when I told what had happened to my then-girlfriend, now-wife, that I realized that a CEO had just physically threatened an employee during a contract dispute.

We drove up the rest of the way in angry silence. I didn't give a shit about the meeting now, as my anger had sealed my decision to leave the company as soon as possible. However, being a professional, I didn't just walk into the president's office and take a dump on his carpet. We went in, Brett either pretending nothing happened or oblivious to how angry I was, and tried to sell the company. Unfortunately, right out the gate, our deal was dead. The president told us he loved the product and was impressed with the work we had done for them already (mostly my own), but due to a statewide budget freeze was unable to purchase it. We talked a little more about the product and what the school needed from us and agreed to reconvene in the next fiscal year, which was only a few months away.

Brett told me I did a good job on the ride home, but there was no saving face. My mind was made up. I was leaving. The next day I went over to Phil's house and told him about our meeting and how on the ride up Brett and I got into an argument about my contract and how he threatened to punch me in the face over it. I told Phil that I was leaving not just because of that, but for a variety of reasons, but added that he needs to keep Brett on a tight leash because if he does that to the wrong person, he's going to get everyone in some serious legal trouble. Phil was very understanding and accepted everything with no pushback. We shook hands and he told me that I was always welcome to come back if I changed my mind.

The next day I went to Brett's house to collect my last paycheck. I created a final invoice tallying up all my unpaid hours, as well as every meeting I had set that had not been paid a bonus. Christina told me to count every single meeting that I had brought us to, whether it was through cold calling or through leveraging my network. I got a nominal amount of money per meeting, I think it was 25 bucks, so I got a couple extra hundred bucks sprinkled on top.

Brett seemed to know that my decision was final, as he did not try to talk me back into working for him when we met up. Perhaps he was just as sick of me as I was of him. I felt that it was necessary to make clear to him how wrong it is to threaten employees when negotiating contract terms and that it was a big part of my decision to leave. Brett apologized, though immediately after apologizing asked me not to tell people what he said. I agreed if only to get out of there. He cut the final check, shook my hand, and

I was gone.

Nine months down the toilet. My savings drained. My budding business in ruins. And all I had to show for it was a $1200 check.

Epilogue

Life after the start-up was tough at first. I was broke and desperate and acutely aware of my lack of prospects. I started trying to rustle up business while selling bags to stay afloat. However, no matter how desperate or hopeless things looked, I swore I would never do business with Brett again. I hoped to never even see him again. Though I didn't feel this way about everyone in the company.

I maintained regular contact with both Christina and Jason. Christina and I would talk on the phone every once in a while. Jason and I would hang out and smoke weed occasionally, though he eventually moved back to California. I kept fronting bags to George and collecting money from him when he sold them, but eventually, our relationship soured when he stiffed me and gave me the runaround. Eventually, weeks after he told me he was too broke to pay me back, I saw he had made some posts on social media about wanting to buy a new video game system, so I sent him a text giving him a hard time about that. He gave me some attitude, though he did offer to pay me an installment, and I declined and told him I was through with him, deciding I'd rather cut my losses than regularly deal with Brett's right-hand man.

I saw Brett a few months later after I had gotten my life more straightened out. I had moved in with my then-girlfriend-now-wife, gotten a job at the mall making custom t-shirts for minimum wage, quit that job, and landed a new job as an office manager for a small company making enough where I could finally quit selling bags. We bumped into each other at a local coffee and bagel spot. I was hoping he wouldn't notice me, but the place was too small for me to escape his attention. He asked how I was doing and I told him I was fine. He asked where I was working now and in the vaguest terms possible told him what I was up to. I made it a point not to ask how the company was doing, though I did ask about his family. He said they were fine then paid for my coffee and then was gone.

I'm not going to pretend I'm not bitter about how things shook out. Frankly, I still think that if managed properly the idea had potential, especially now with Covid shaking up the business world. But Brett was not the person to make it happen. It was not meant to be. I won't go as far as to say that I was glad this all happened to me, but I will confess that my time working for a "true startup" was an invaluable experience. I learned a great deal about sales, how to build a business, and what good leadership looks like. Moreover, I also experienced a painful lesson in letting greed cloud judgment. There were a million warning signs that this company was going to fall apart at the seams. I was ignorant of many of them at the time but looking back there were questions that I did not know to ask as well as ones that I didn't want to ask. Additionally, I was also unaware of my own leverage and what my worth was, which is something I might not have ever learned if I hadn't gone through this experience.

I guess the biggest lesson here is that risks must be properly assessed with a clear head and good judgment. Promises of potential wealth are intoxicating, but greed is irrational and will bend us into all sorts of positions that make us ignore every red flag we see. Likewise, going into business with friends or acquaintances is something that should be carefully considered, since our love for our friends similarly clouds our judgment. To put it simply, fortune favors the bold, but bold does not mean stupid.

About the Author

Photo by Kathleen Castro (Edited by Mick Theebs)

Mick Theebs lives in southern Connecticut. He has since recovered from his start-up experience. More of his writing can be found in his poetry collection *Somnambulist* and his satirical play *Hamlet 2020*. When he is not writing, Mick enjoys cooking, gardening, and playing with his dogs Yoshi and Mr. Pugsley. Yes, those are their real names.

To stay up to date on what Mick is doing, follow him on Twitter (if it even still exists anymore) @MickTheebs and visit his website www.micktheebs.com.

More of his writing can be found on Chaotic Order, his Medium publication.

More Titles by Mick Theebs

Somnambulist

Hamlet 2020

Laureate

www.ingramcontent.com/pod-product-compliance
Lightning Source LLC
Chambersburg PA
CBHW031209090426
42736CB00009B/842